# ANATOMY Coloring Book

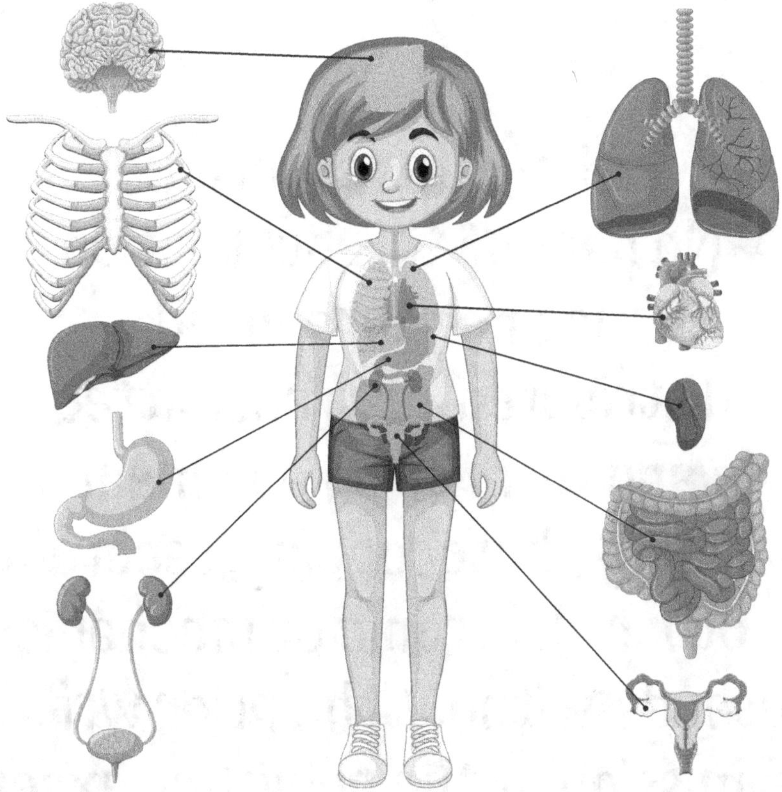

## This Book Belongs To

---

---

---

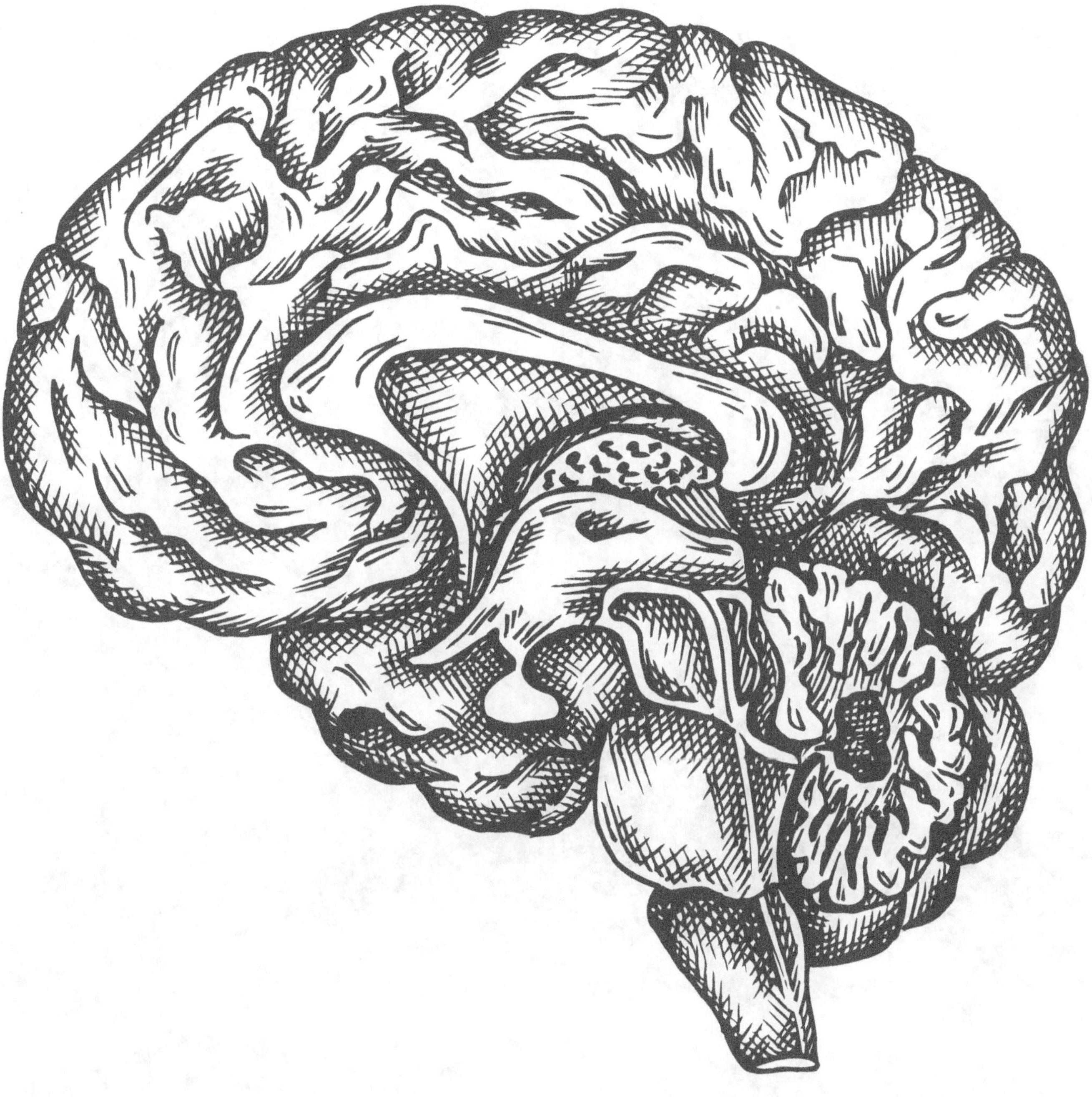

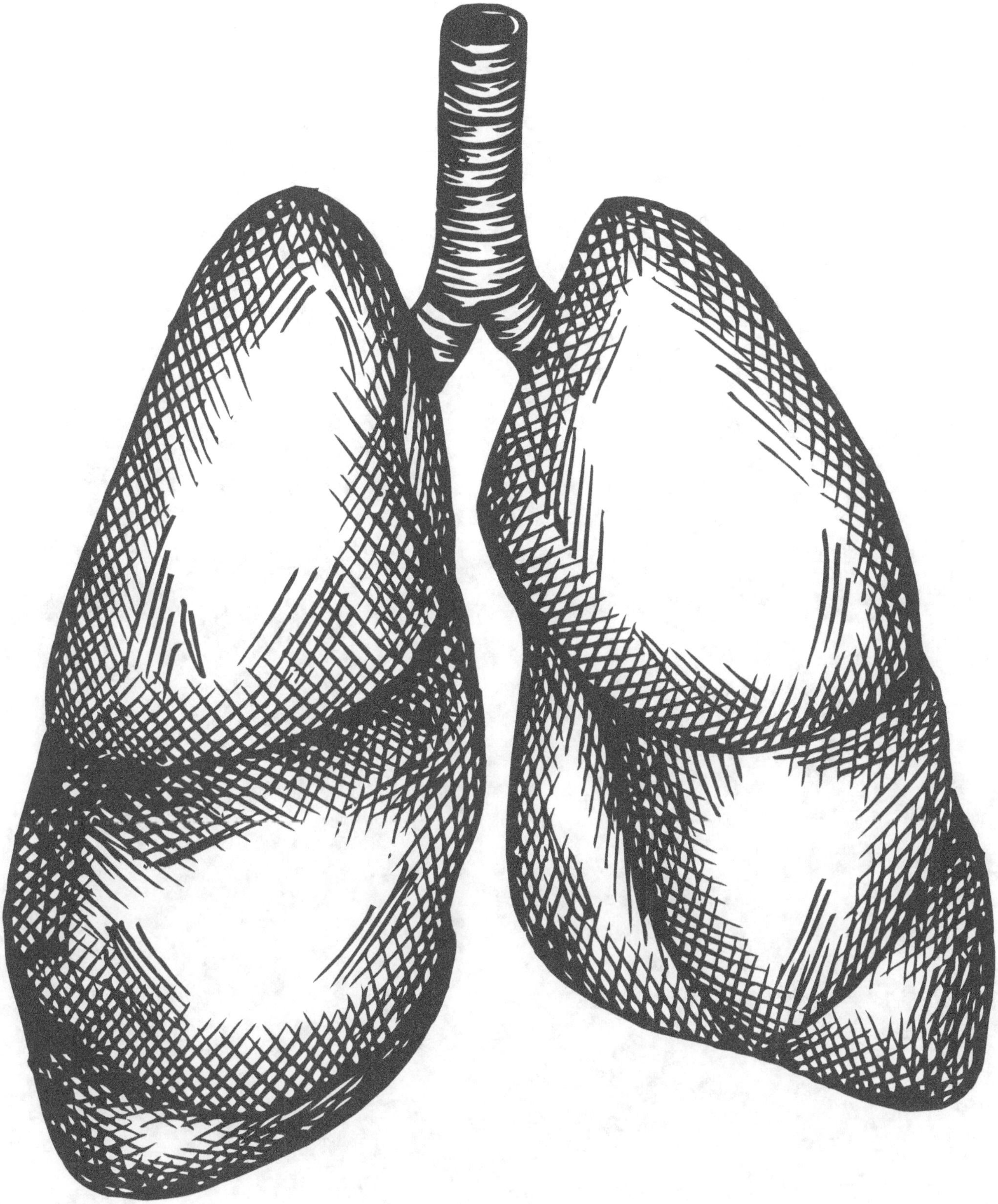

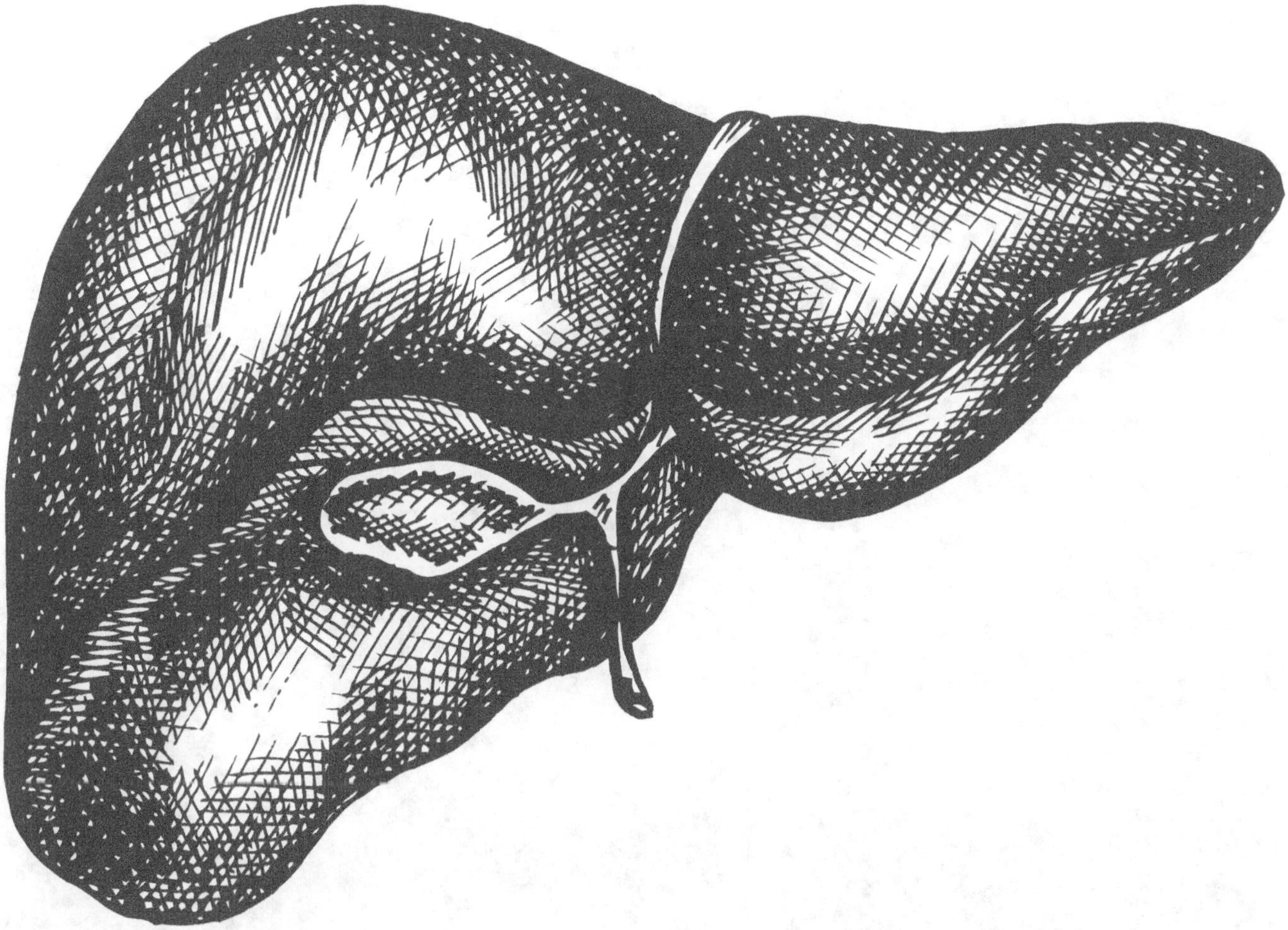

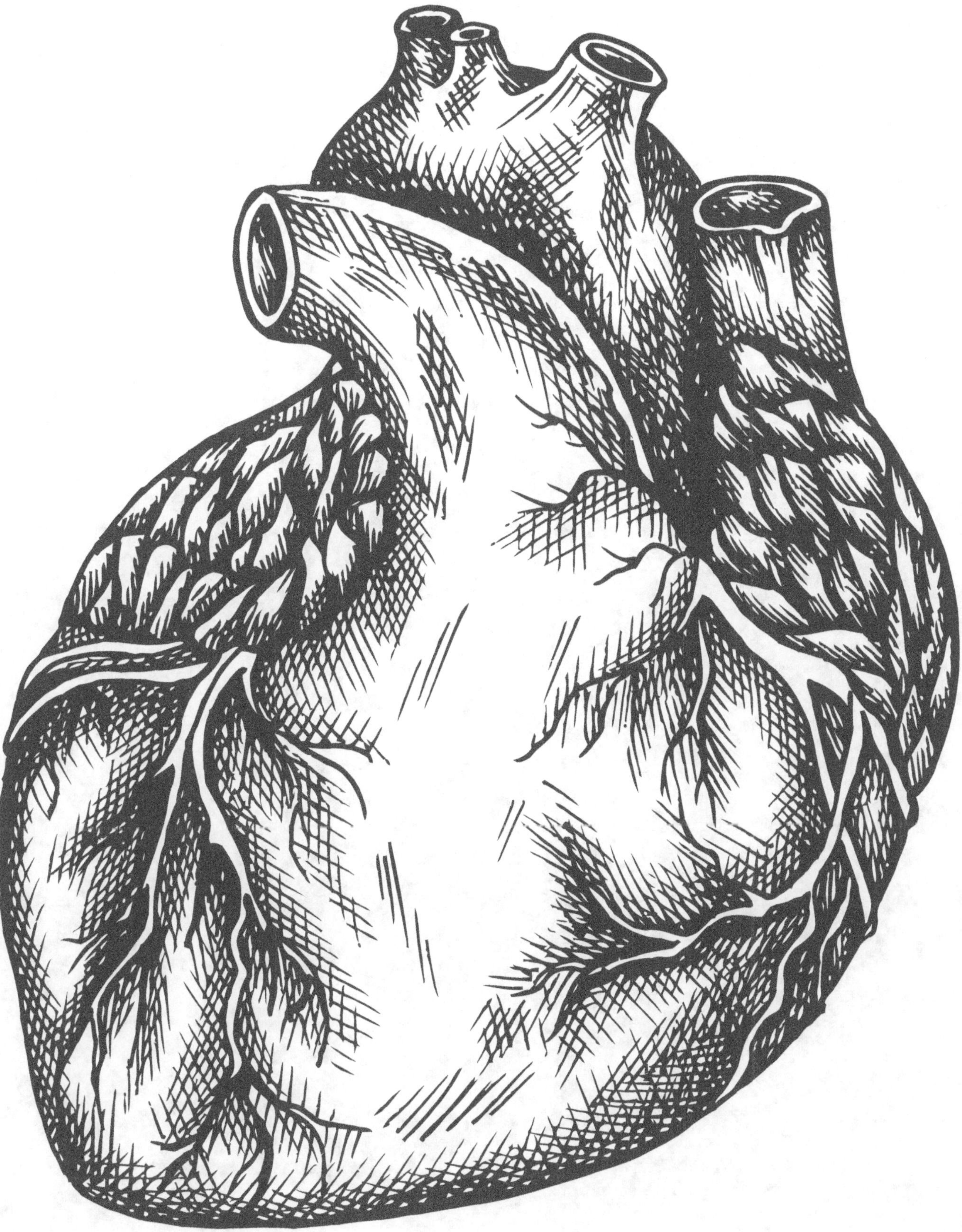

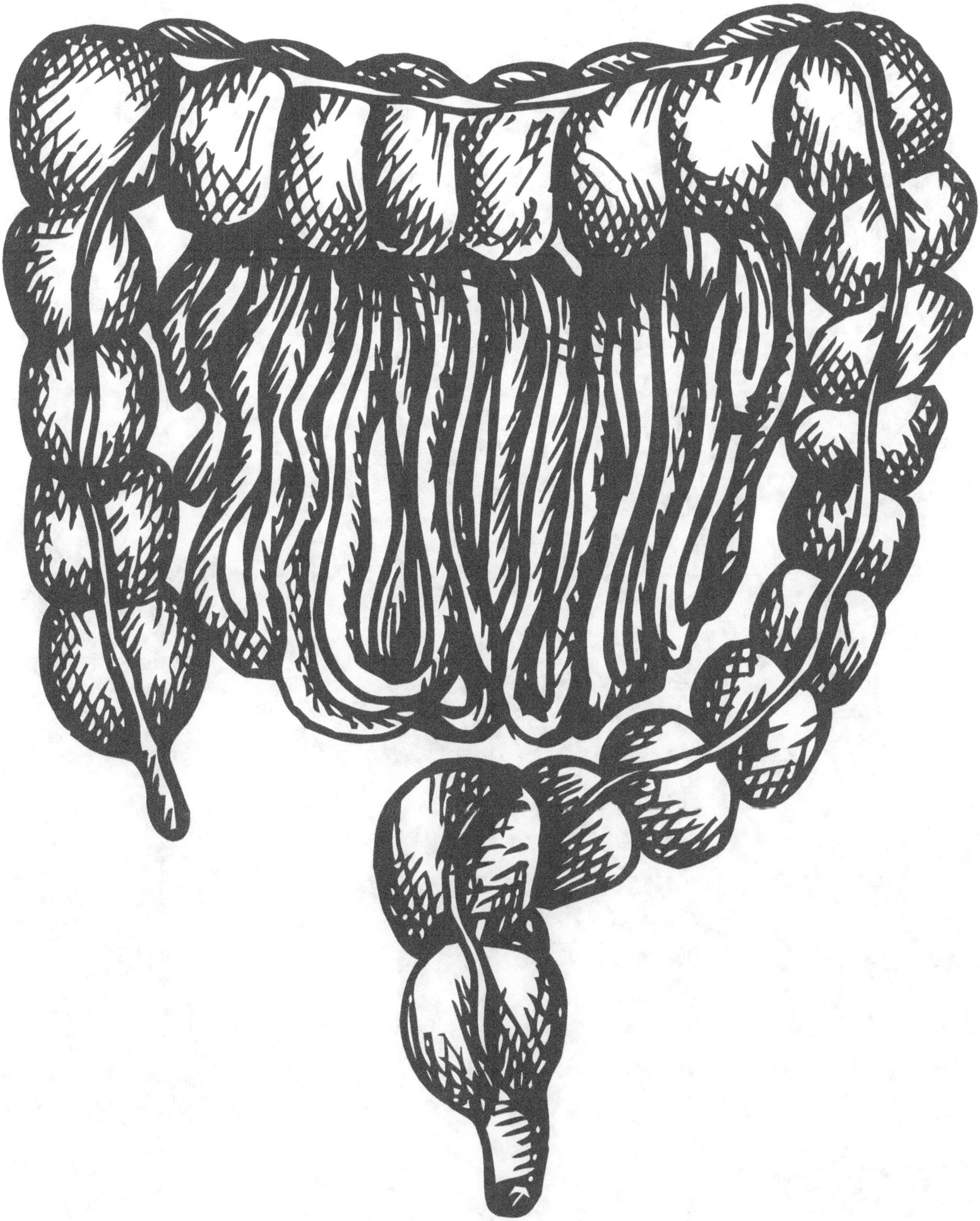

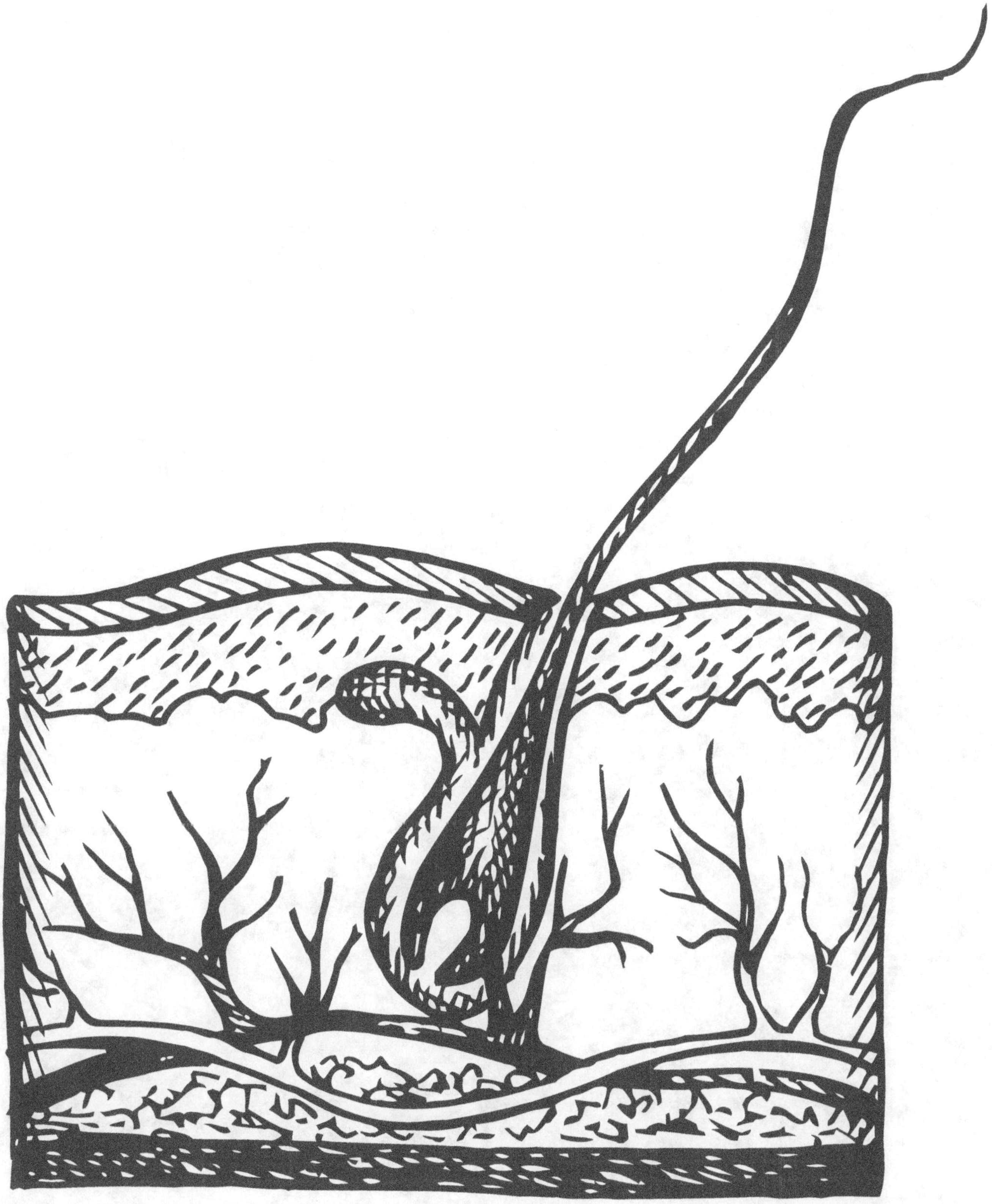

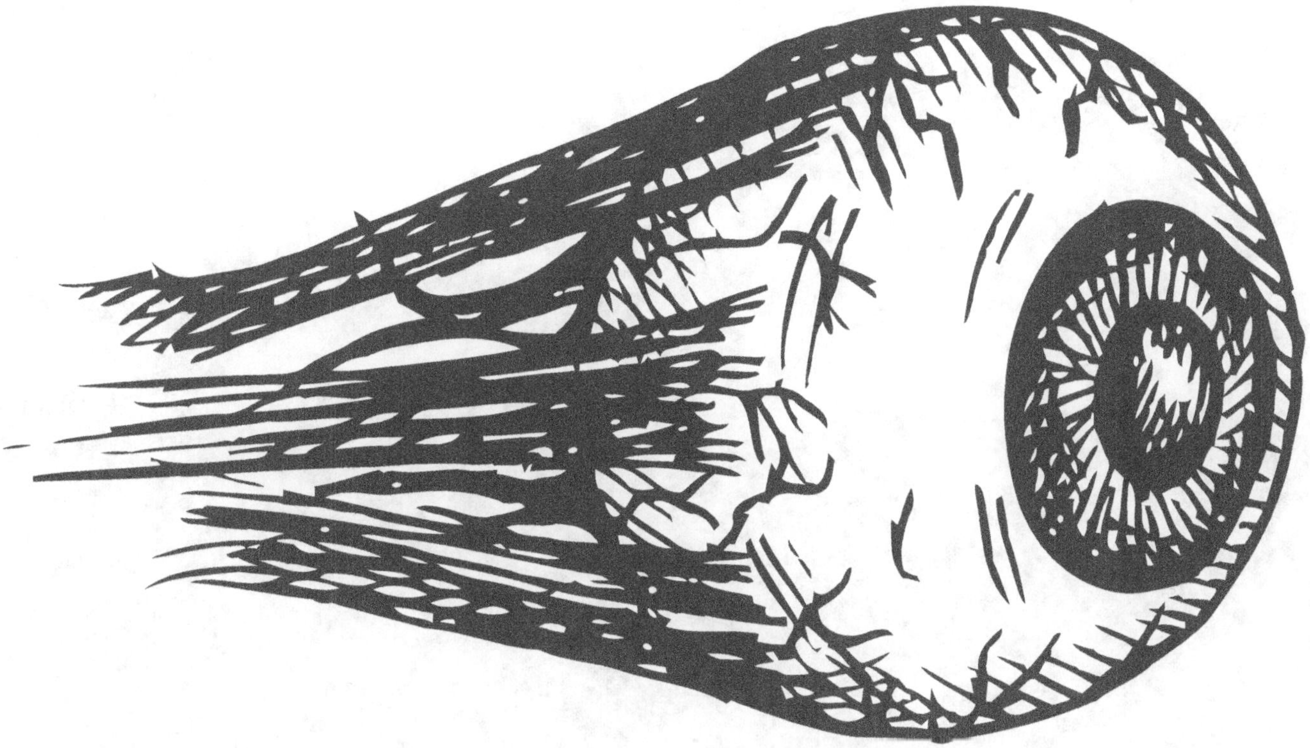

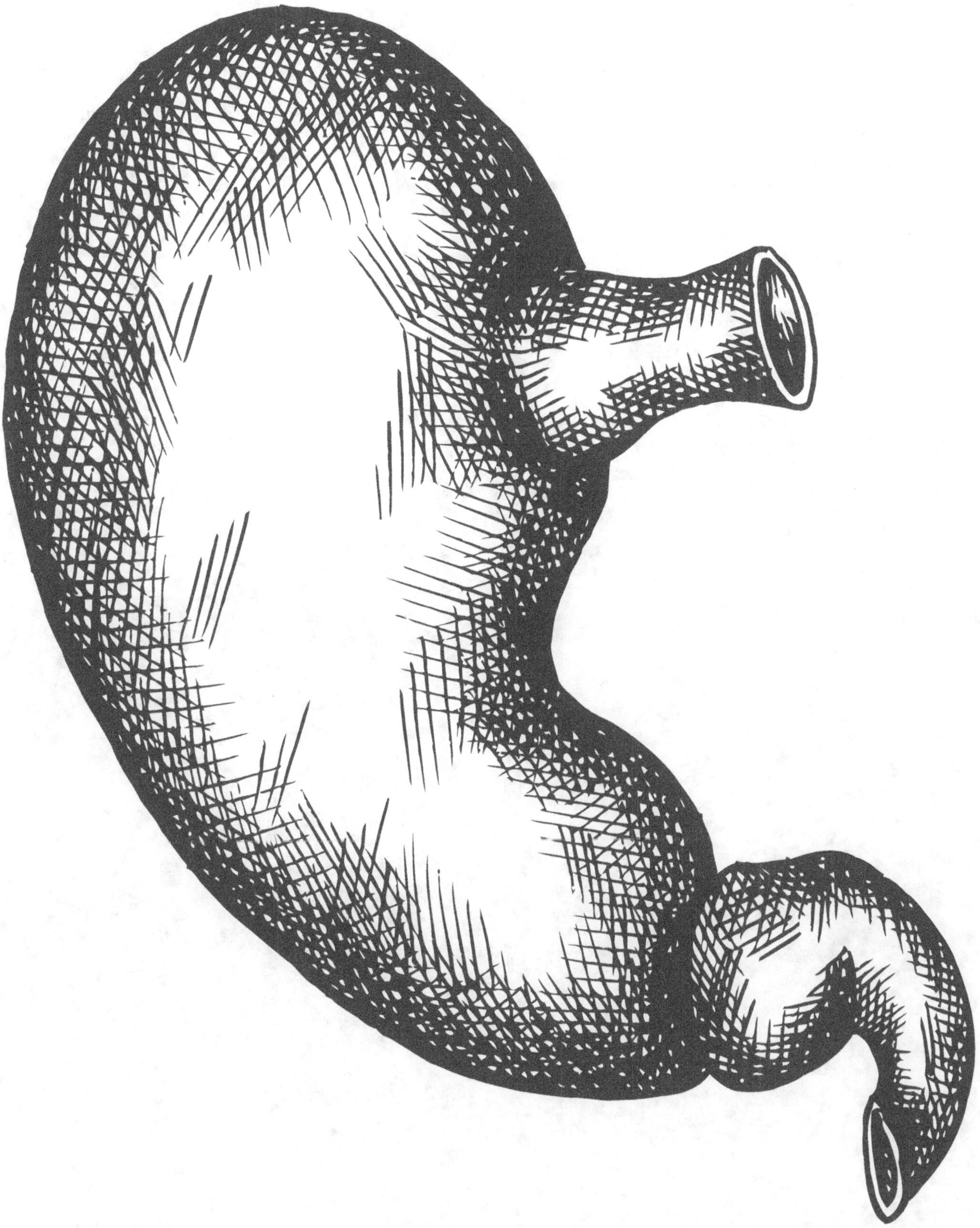

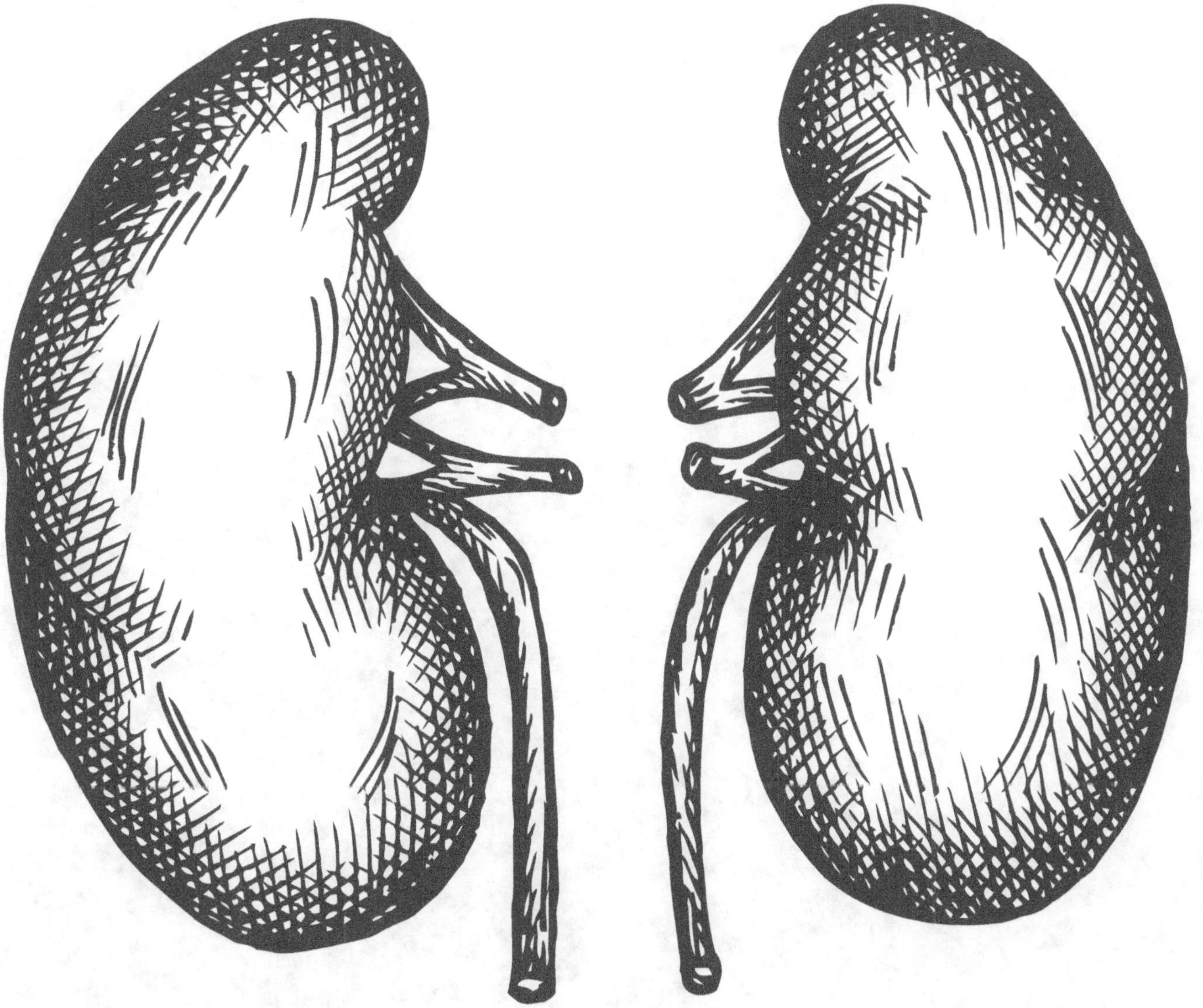

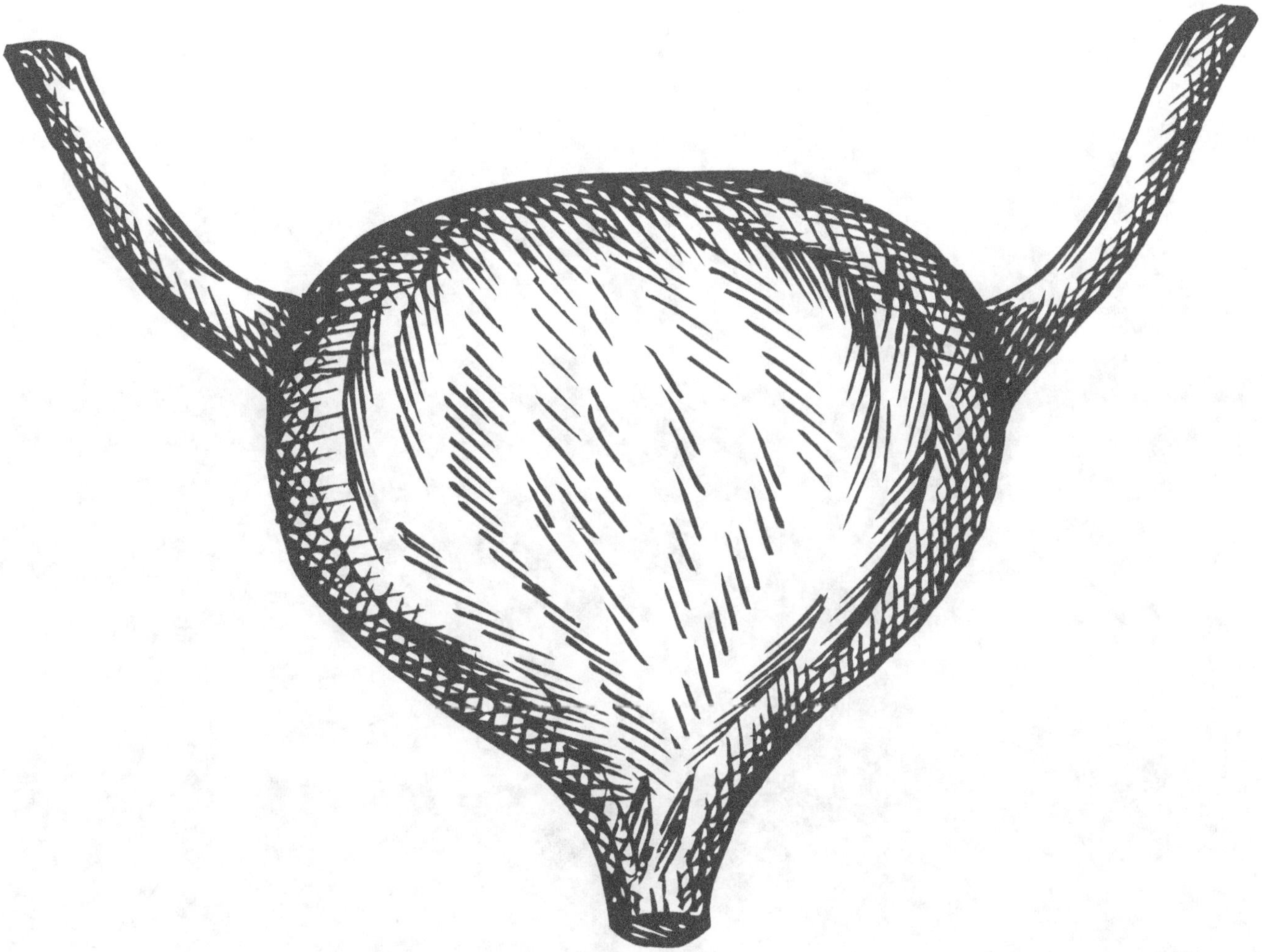

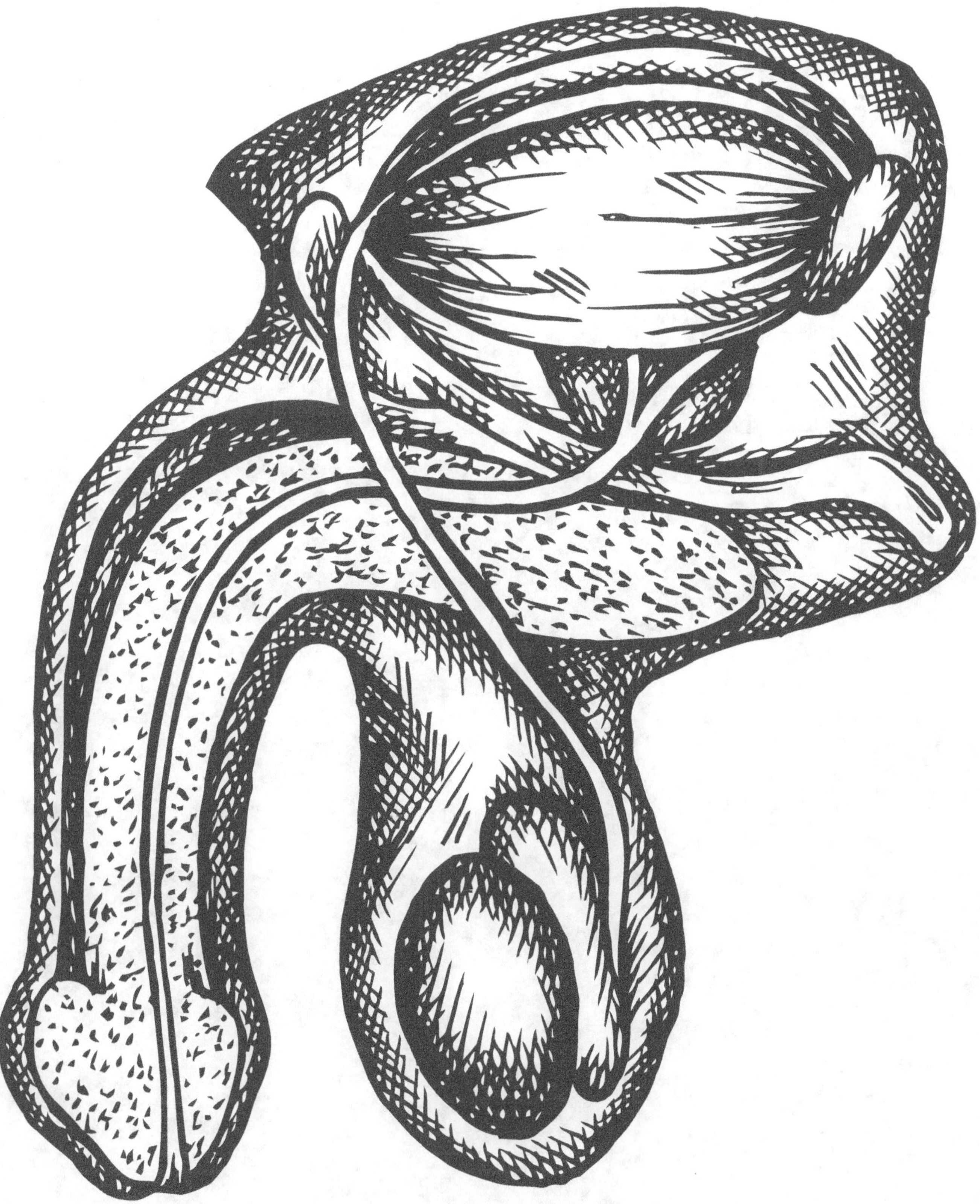

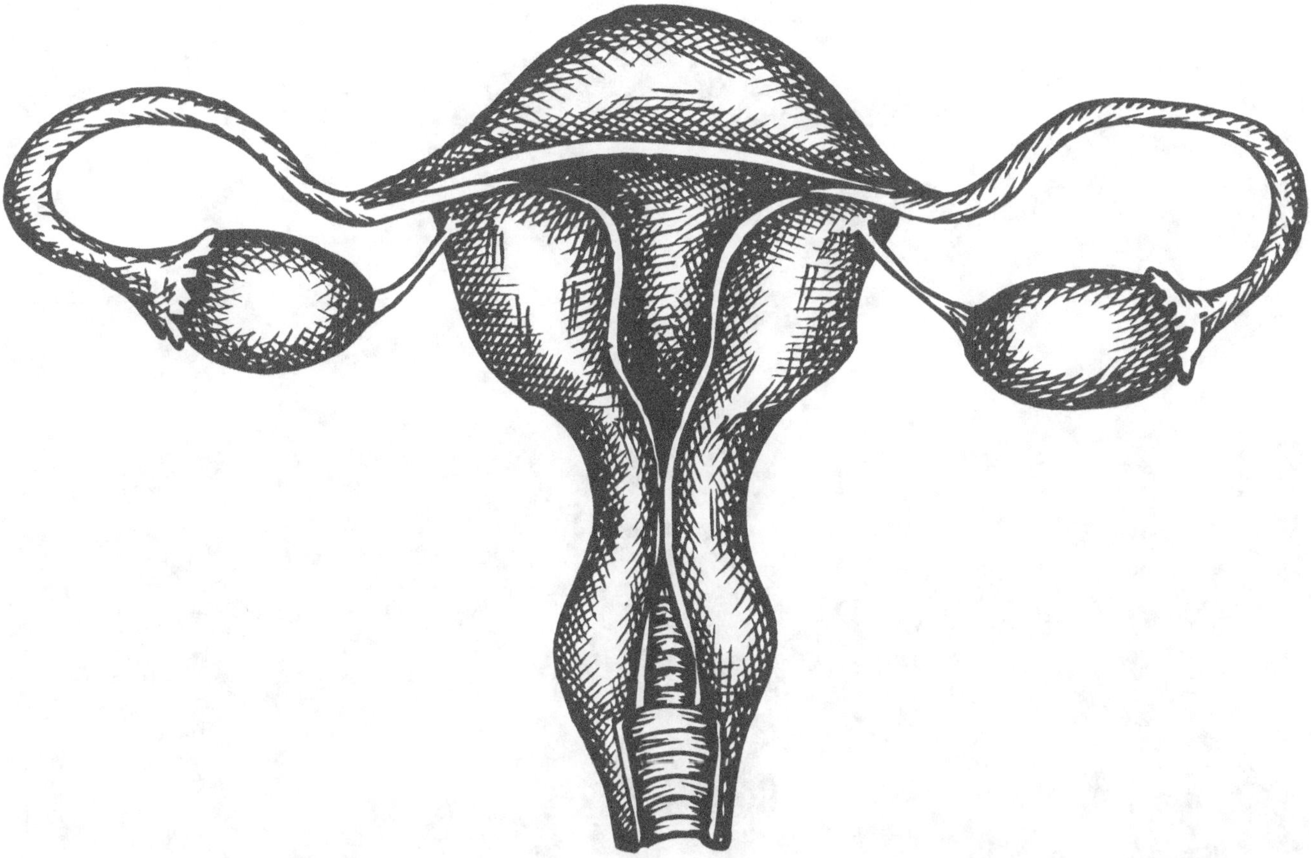

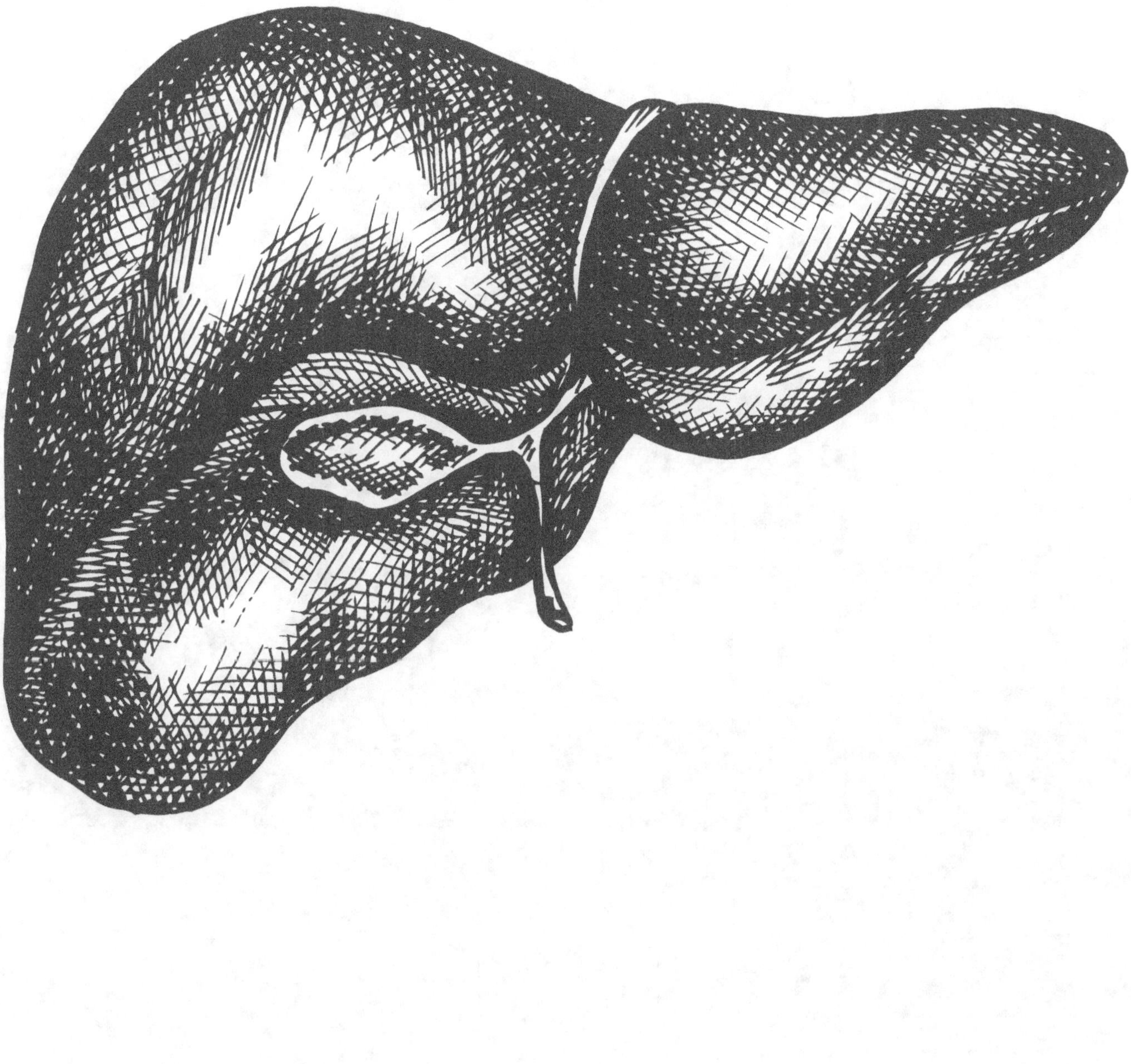

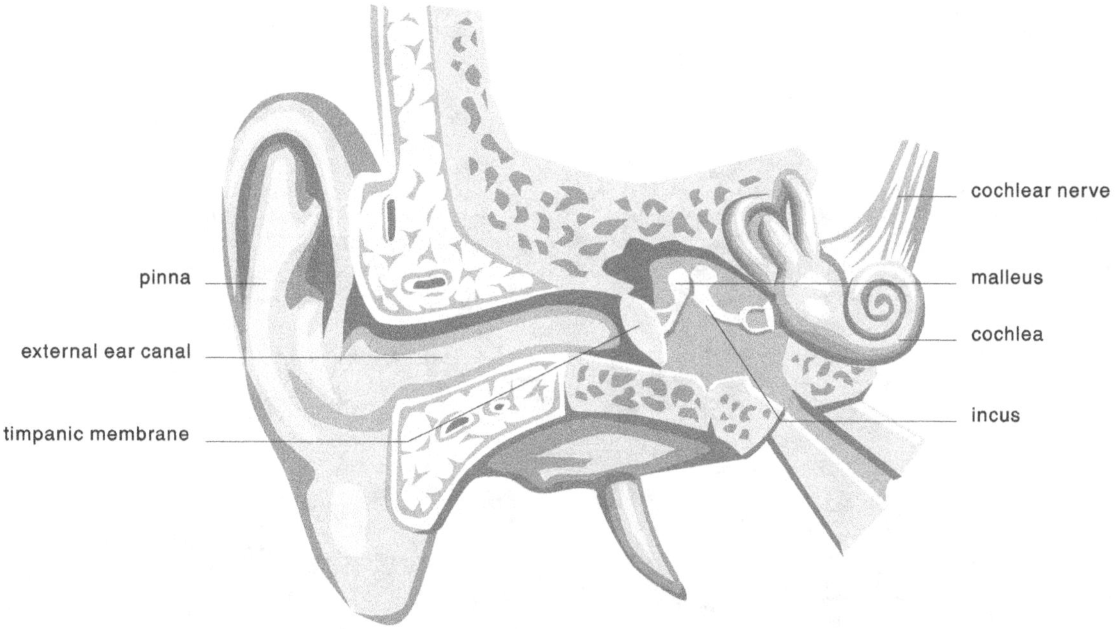
cochlear nerve
pinna
malleus
cochlea
external ear canal
incus
timpanic membrane

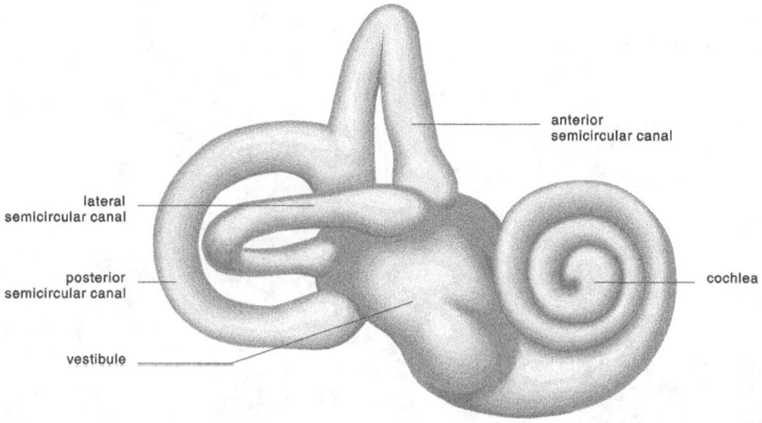
anterior
semicircular canal
lateral
semicircular canal
posterior
semicircular canal
cochlea
vestibule

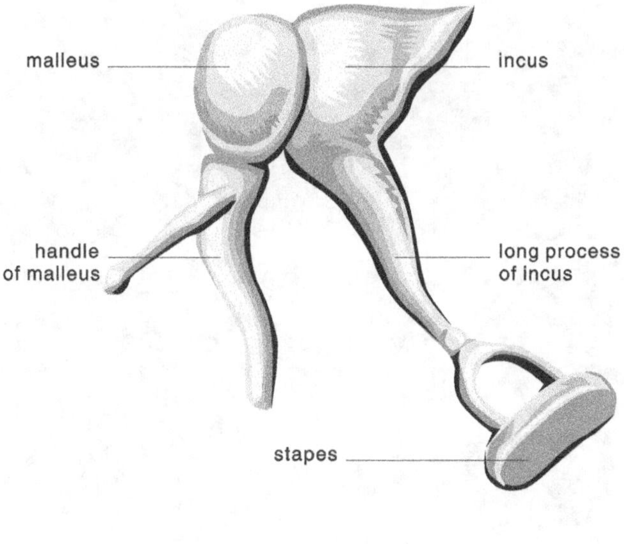
malleus
incus
handle
of malleus
long process
of incus
stapes

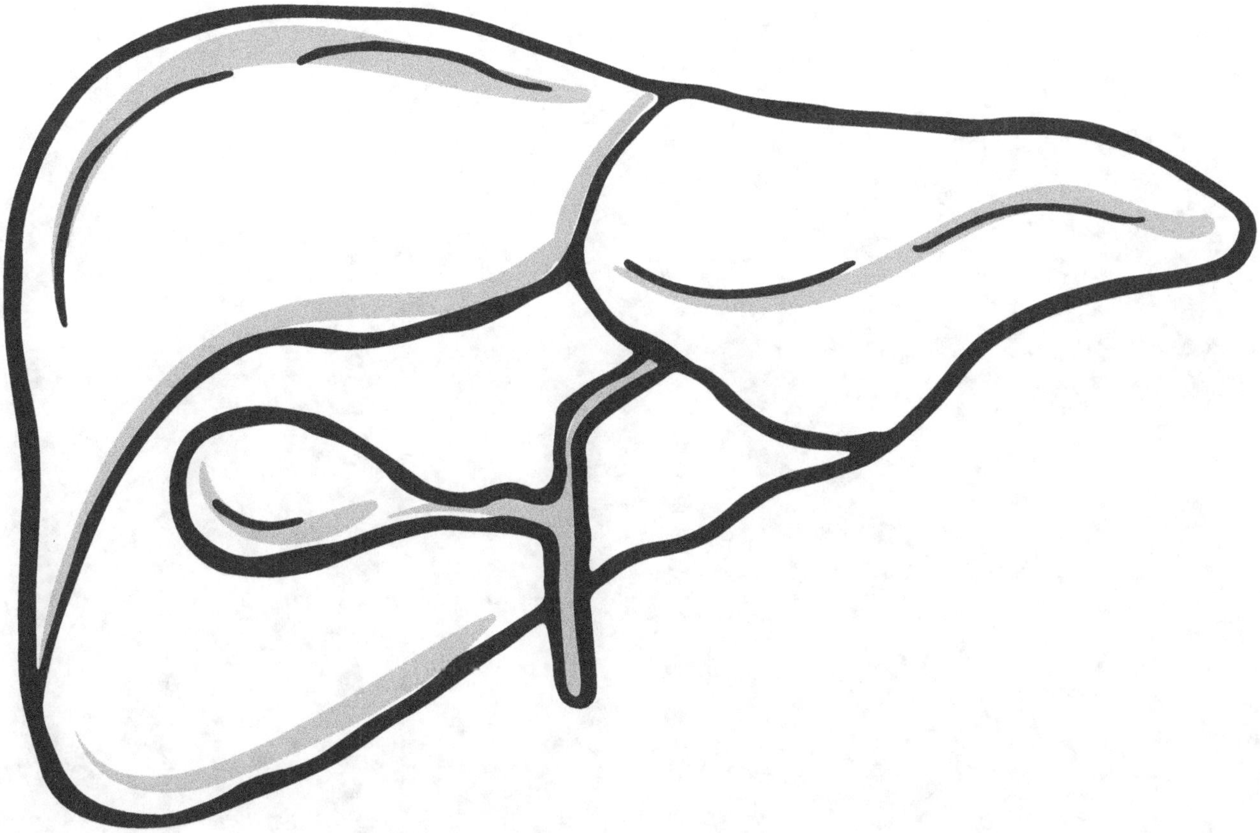

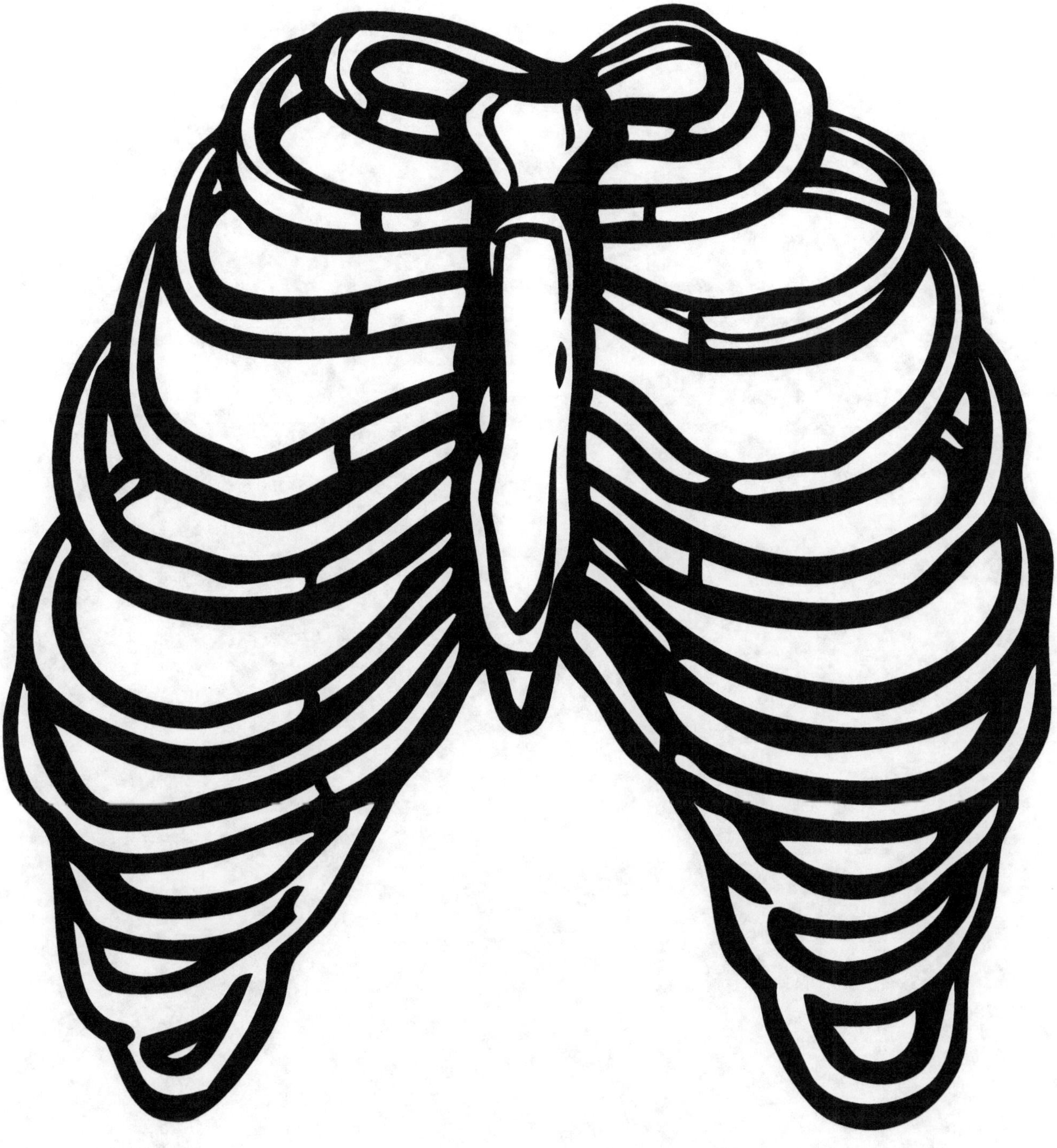

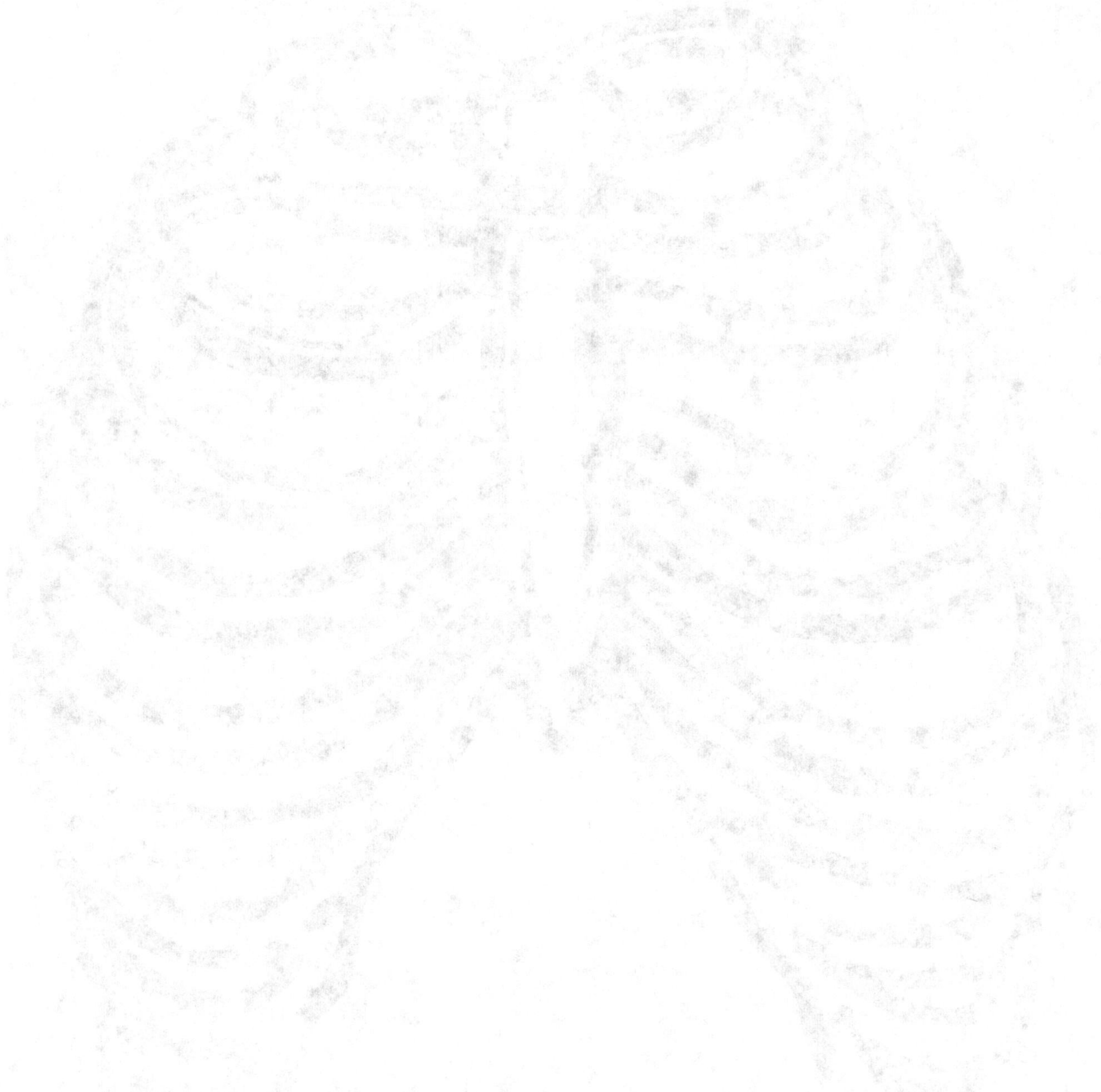

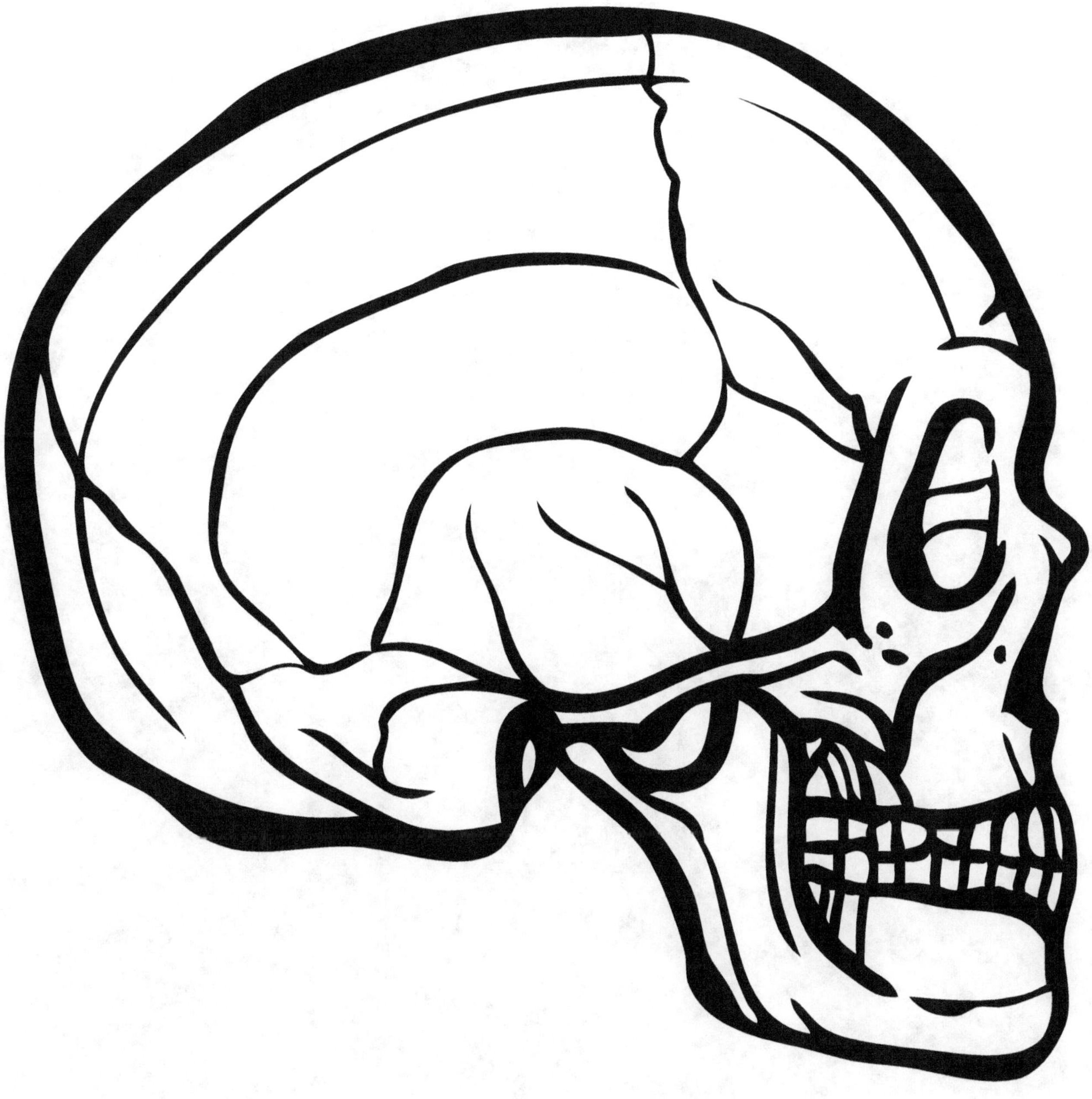

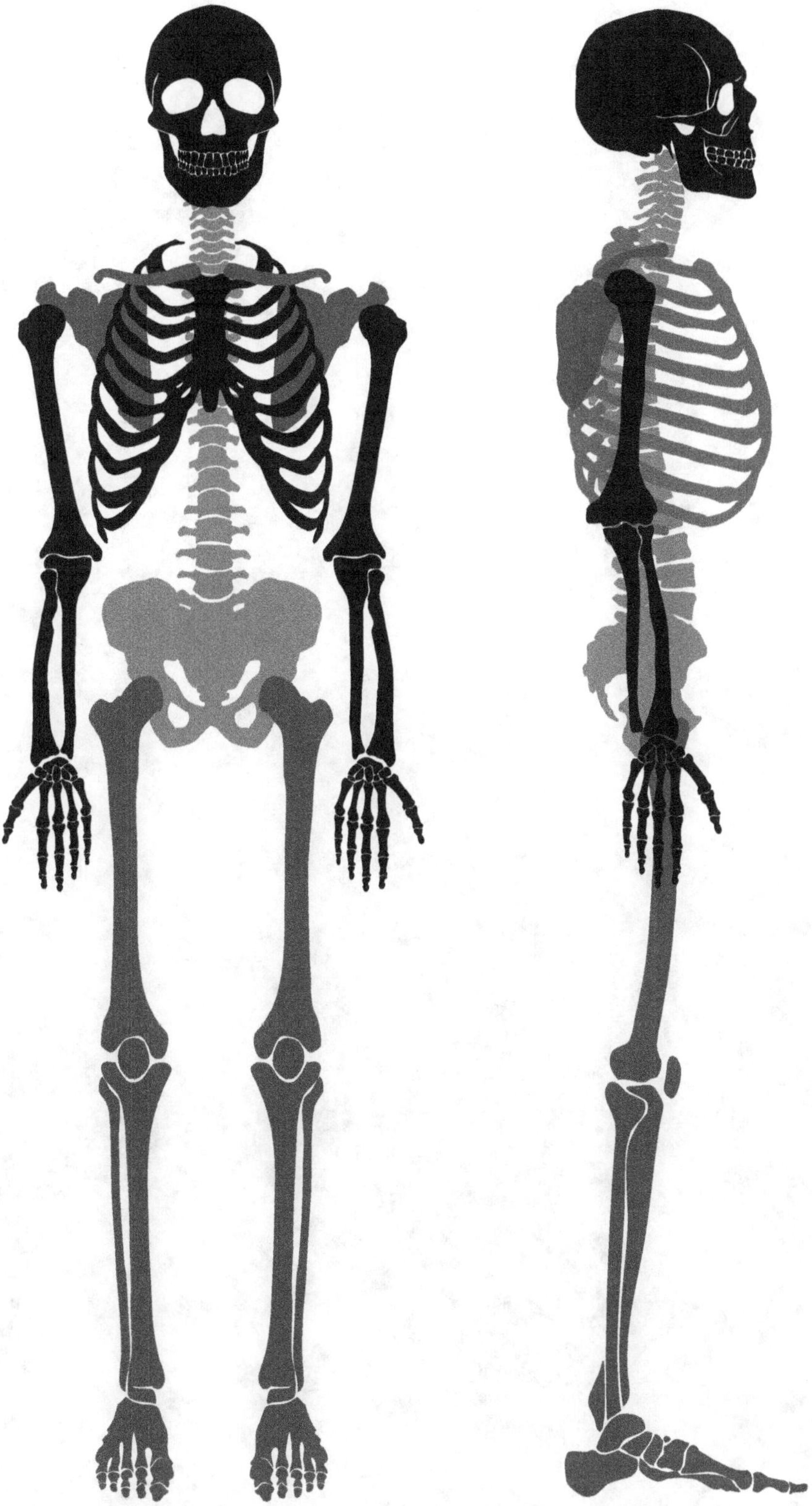

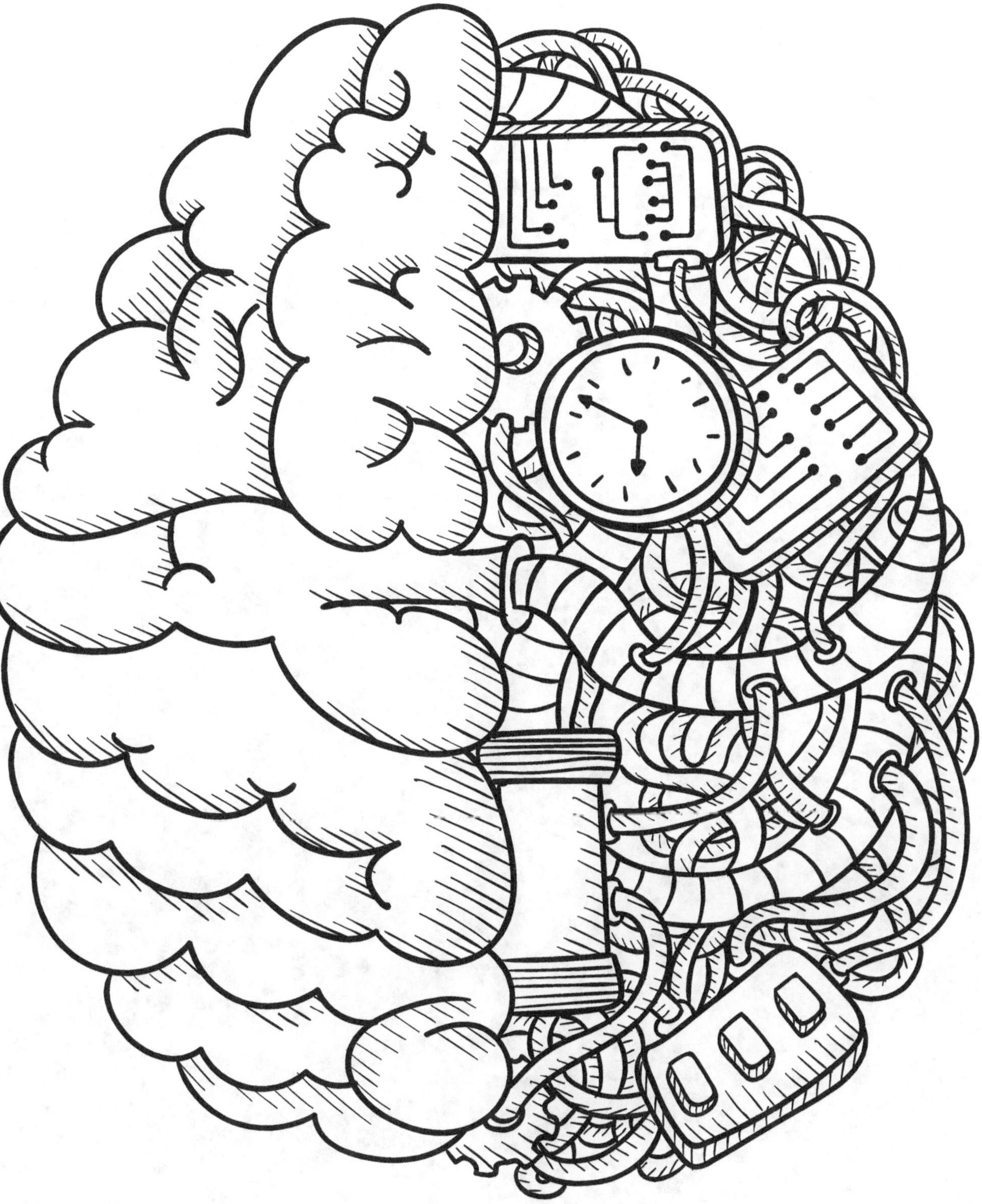

www.ingramcontent.com/pod-product-compliance
Lightning Source LLC
Chambersburg PA
CBHW081543220526
45467CB00010B/3302
* 9 7 8 1 7 0 4 9 7 4 0 4 0 *